Designed by Flowerpot Press
www.FlowerpotPress.com
CHC-0909-0524
ISBN: 978-1-4867-2277-8
Made in China/Fabriqué en Chine

HOW DO SATELLITES STAY IN SPACE?

A BOOK ABOUT HOW SATELLITES WORK

TV   Radio

written by jessica taylor

illustrated by srimalie bassani

It's a bird! It's a plane! It's a satellite!

Have you ever noticed a tiny bright light moving across the sky? If so, you may have seen a satellite. A satellite is something in space, a natural or human-made object, that goes around a bigger object. The moon is considered a satellite since it goes around Earth.

Moon

Earth

The universe is full of spectacular things!

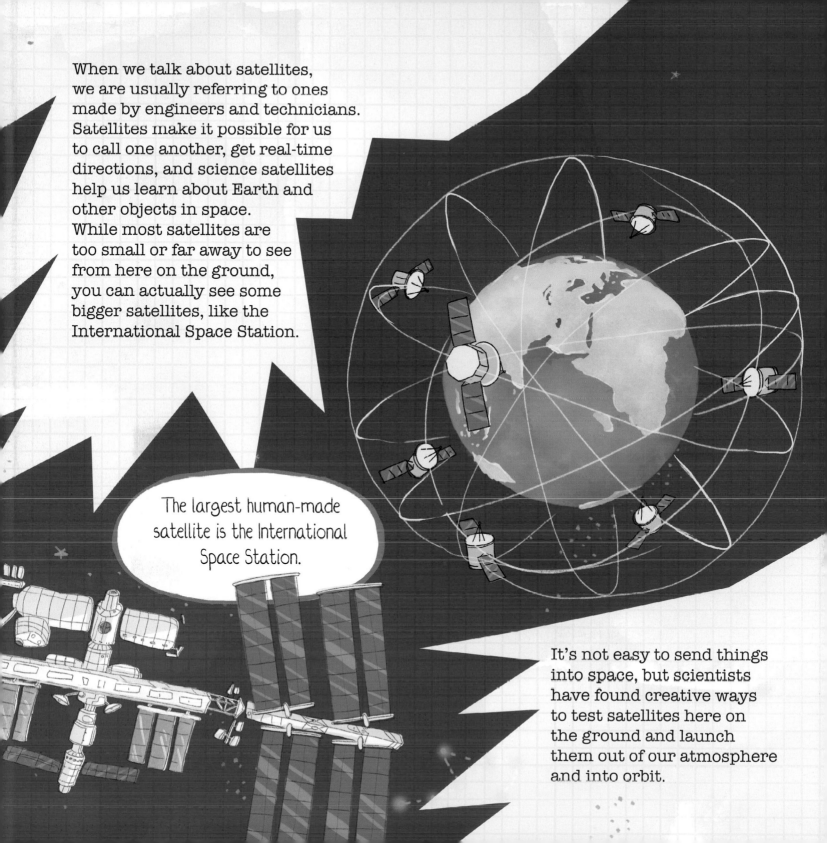

When we talk about satellites, we are usually referring to ones made by engineers and technicians. Satellites make it possible for us to call one another, get real-time directions, and science satellites help us learn about Earth and other objects in space. While most satellites are too small or far away to see from here on the ground, you can actually see some bigger satellites, like the International Space Station.

The largest human-made satellite is the International Space Station.

It's not easy to send things into space, but scientists have found creative ways to test satellites here on the ground and launch them out of our atmosphere and into orbit.

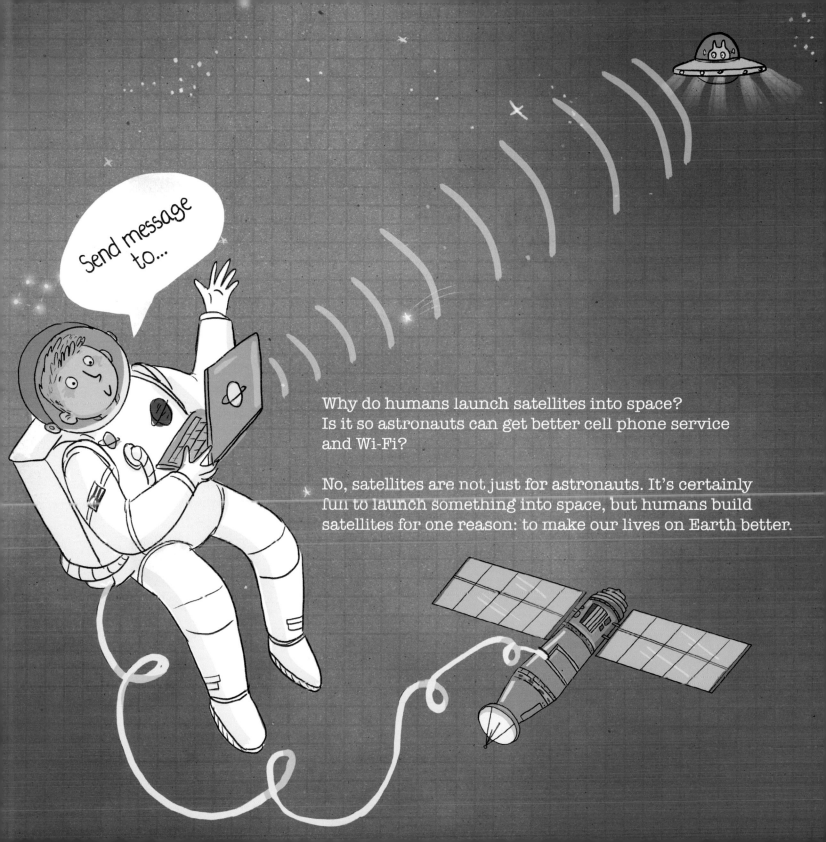

Why do humans launch satellites into space?
Is it so astronauts can get better cell phone service
and Wi-Fi?

No, satellites are not just for astronauts. It's certainly
fun to launch something into space, but humans build
satellites for one reason: to make our lives on Earth better.

Satellites help us to connect with our technology, like our TVs, phones, computers, radios, and GPS systems!

Satellites connect people to one another through communication and facilitate entertainment by providing television signals. They even help us get around down here on Earth by supplying us with navigation information, like the maps you use on a phone to find your friend's house.

Satellites also use the unique perspective from space to monitor Earth and with the help of an instrument onboard, a satellite can measure the environment here on the ground. For example, satellites help measure things like rainfall, sea levels, the greenness of leaves, and even track air pollution. While some satellites focus on gathering information about Earth, others help us learn about amazing things in space, like our moon, Mars, and even distant galaxies.

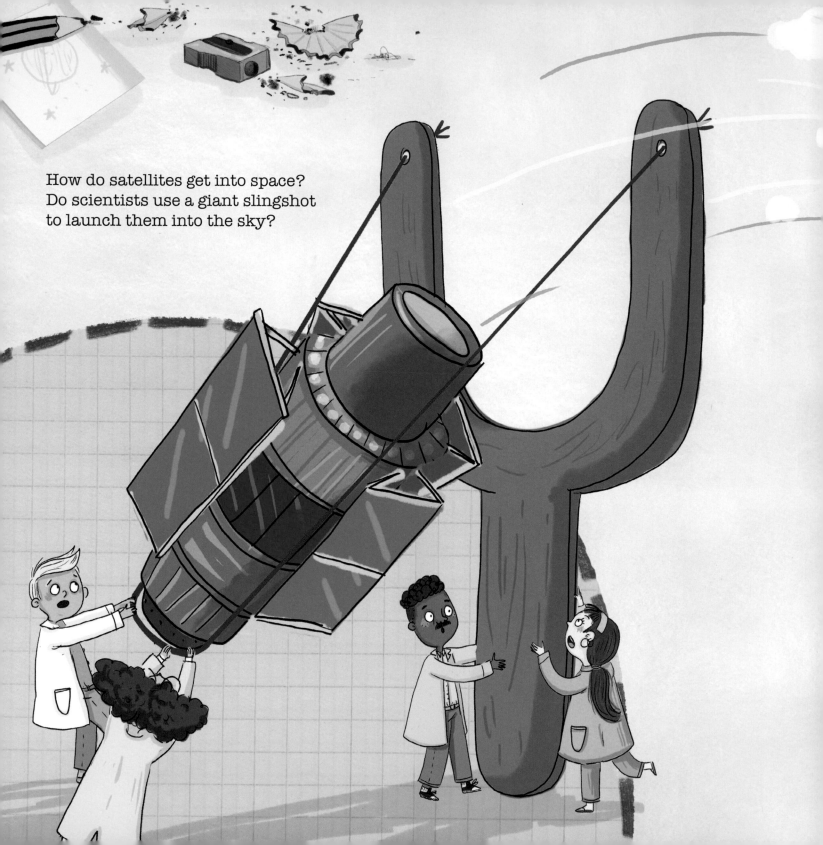

How do satellites get into space?
Do scientists use a giant slingshot
to launch them into the sky?

No, scientists don't use a giant slingshot, but they do use rockets! Satellites get launched into space by hitching a ride on a rocket.

A rocket blasts off from Earth at an extreme speed, over 17,500 miles (28,163.5 kilometers) per hour, to leave our atmosphere and travel into space. Once the rocket reaches the right distance away from Earth, the satellite separates from the rocket.

HOW DO SATELLITES GET TO SPACE?

fairing

spacecraft

second stage

first stage

payload attach fitting

solid motor rockets

interstage

fairing

centerbody section

Satellite Communications
Systems Engineering

How satellites get into space is a great example of the Law of Inertia—an object in motion will stay in motion. The satellite moves in the direction it was traveling while attached to the rocket and once it separates it is pulled down slightly by Earth's gravity. This allows the satellite to travel on a curved path and orbit Earth.

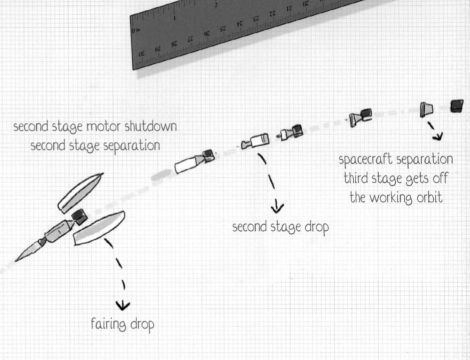

second stage motor shutdown
second stage separation

spacecraft separation
third stage gets off
the working orbit

second stage drop

fairing drop

second stage motor ignited

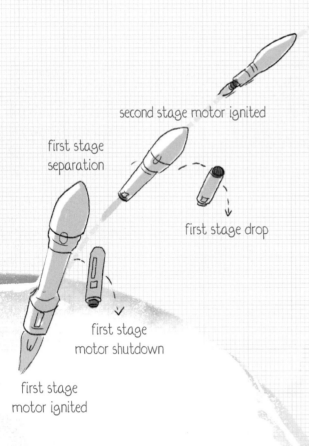

first stage
separation

first stage drop

first stage
motor shutdown

first stage
motor ignited

So now the satellite is in space, but what happens to the rocket? Rockets are a transportation vehicle. Rockets can also carry other things into space, like astronauts or cargo for the International Space Station. Just like a bus, rockets may carry multiple payloads, which can be thought of like passengers. Rockets are big and require a lot of fuel, called propellant, to thrust them into space. As a rocket reaches various stages on its journey, it begins to shed pieces that are no longer necessary. Sometimes pieces from the rocket burn up upon re-entry or pieces will fall back down to Earth and into the ocean to be recovered later. But engineers have now been able to develop reusable rockets that are able to come down safely onto land.

The satellite uses the energy it picked up from the rocket to stay in motion. That motion is called momentum.

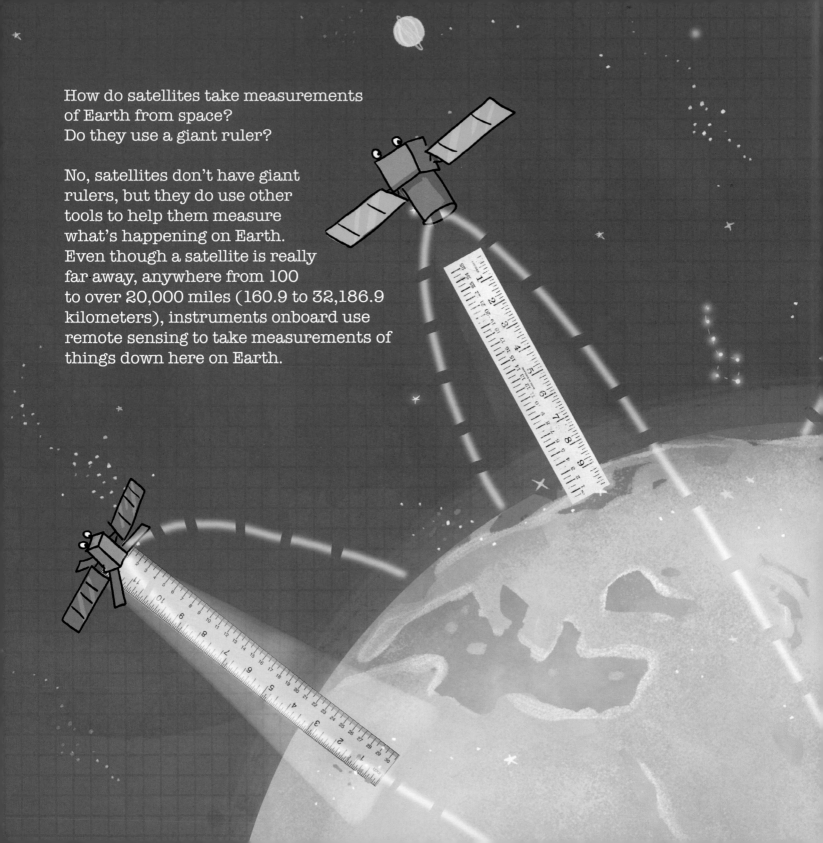

How do satellites take measurements
of Earth from space?
Do they use a giant ruler?

No, satellites don't have giant
rulers, but they do use other
tools to help them measure
what's happening on Earth.
Even though a satellite is really
far away, anywhere from 100
to over 20,000 miles (160.9 to 32,186.9
kilometers), instruments onboard use
remote sensing to take measurements of
things down here on Earth.

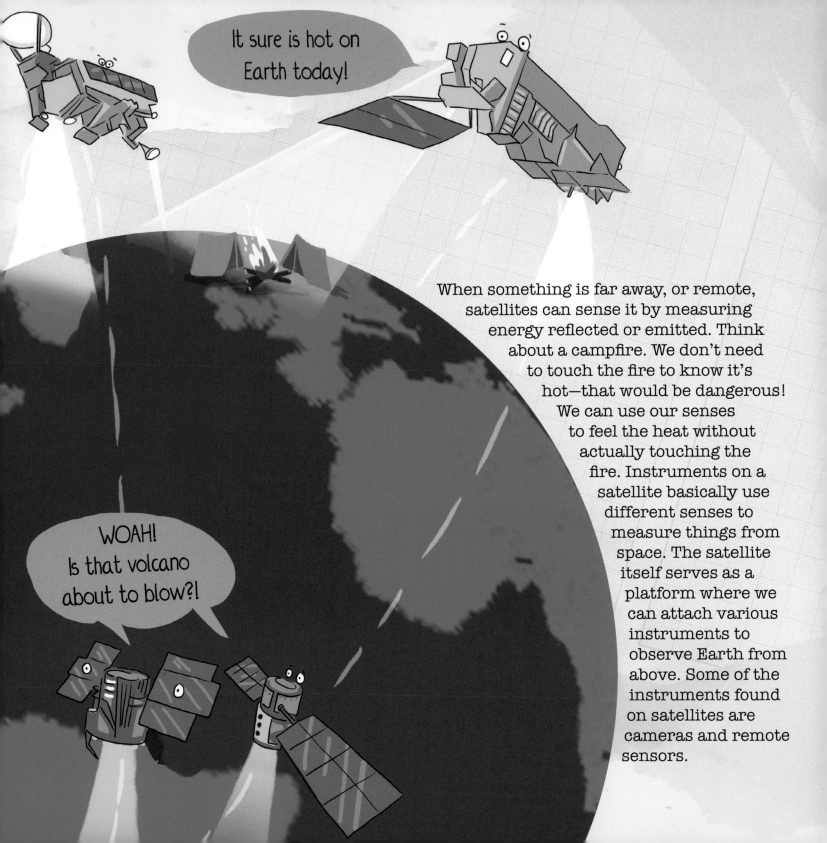

It sure is hot on Earth today!

When something is far away, or remote, satellites can sense it by measuring energy reflected or emitted. Think about a campfire. We don't need to touch the fire to know it's hot—that would be dangerous! We can use our senses to feel the heat without actually touching the fire. Instruments on a satellite basically use different senses to measure things from space. The satellite itself serves as a platform where we can attach various instruments to observe Earth from above. Some of the instruments found on satellites are cameras and remote sensors.

WOAH! Is that volcano about to blow?!

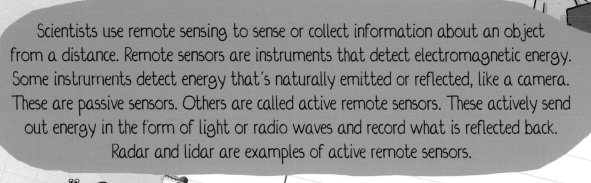

Scientists use remote sensing to sense or collect information about an object from a distance. Remote sensors are instruments that detect electromagnetic energy. Some instruments detect energy that's naturally emitted or reflected, like a camera. These are passive sensors. Others are called active remote sensors. These actively send out energy in the form of light or radio waves and record what is reflected back. Radar and lidar are examples of active remote sensors.

HOW SATELLITE REMOTE SENSORS CAN HELP

- They can take pictures of bigger areas of the Earth's surface to provide scientists with more data.

- They can capture large forest fires so rangers can see the extent of the fires.

- They can track clouds to help predict weather patterns, dust storms, and even volcano eruptions.

- They can take many photos over time to track population growth and changes in cities, farmland, and forests over several years or even decades.

- They can help discover and map parts of the ocean floor.

Did you know radar and lidar are actually acronyms? (Radio Detection and Ranging and Light Detection and Ranging)

How do scientists get information back from satellites?
Do satellites send carrier pigeons to Earth with the data they collect?

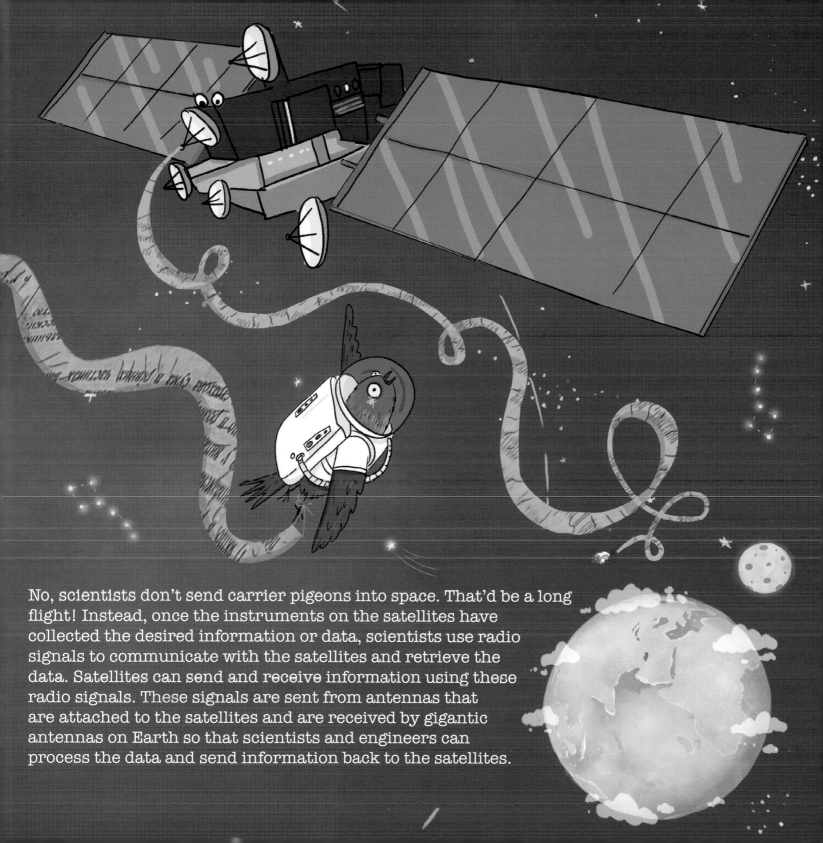

No, scientists don't send carrier pigeons into space. That'd be a long flight! Instead, once the instruments on the satellites have collected the desired information or data, scientists use radio signals to communicate with the satellites and retrieve the data. Satellites can send and receive information using these radio signals. These signals are sent from antennas that are attached to the satellites and are received by gigantic antennas on Earth so that scientists and engineers can process the data and send information back to the satellites.

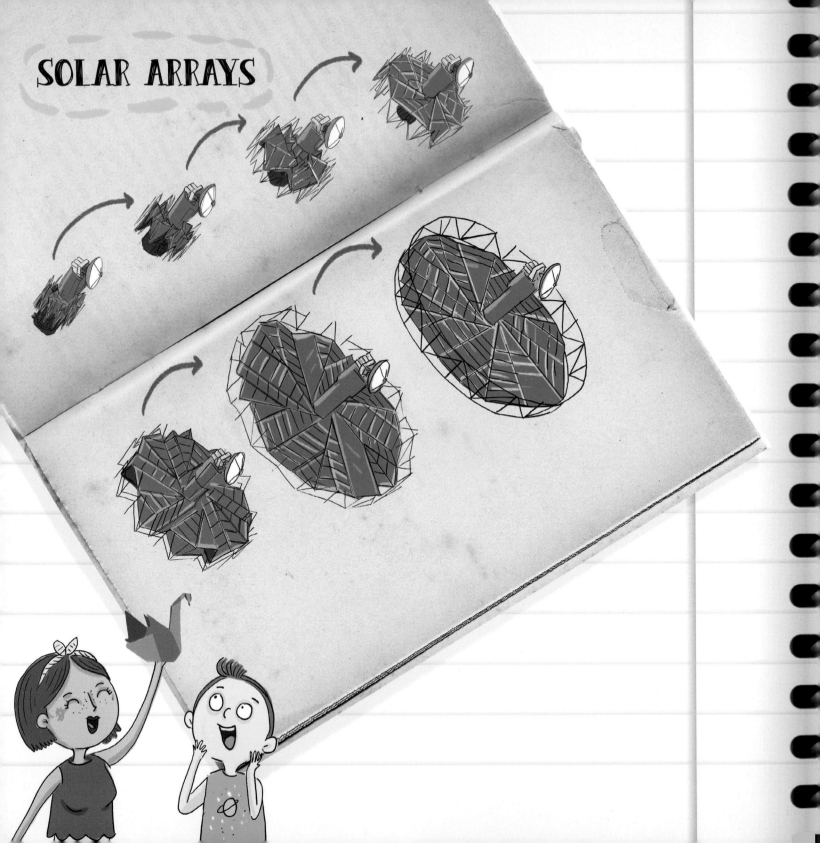

SOLAR ARRAYS

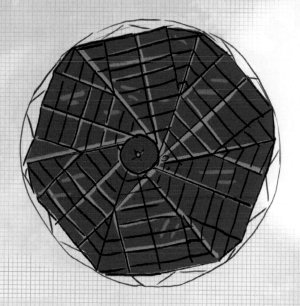

In order for the antennas on the satellite to function, they need power. Since you can't just plug a satellite into an electrical outlet in space, it needs to be able to produce its own power. It does this by using solar power. The satellites get solar power via the solar arrays on a satellite. The solar arrays that are attached to them can be very large, depending on the size of the satellite and location in space. When a satellite is being launched on a rocket, it must be as small as possible. Because of their size, the solar arrays on a satellite are folded in when the satellite is launched on the rocket and then they unfold when the satellite is in orbit, kind of like an origami swan.

How do satellites avoid hitting other satellites or space junk in space?
Do they wear inflatable floaties to protect them if they bump into one another?

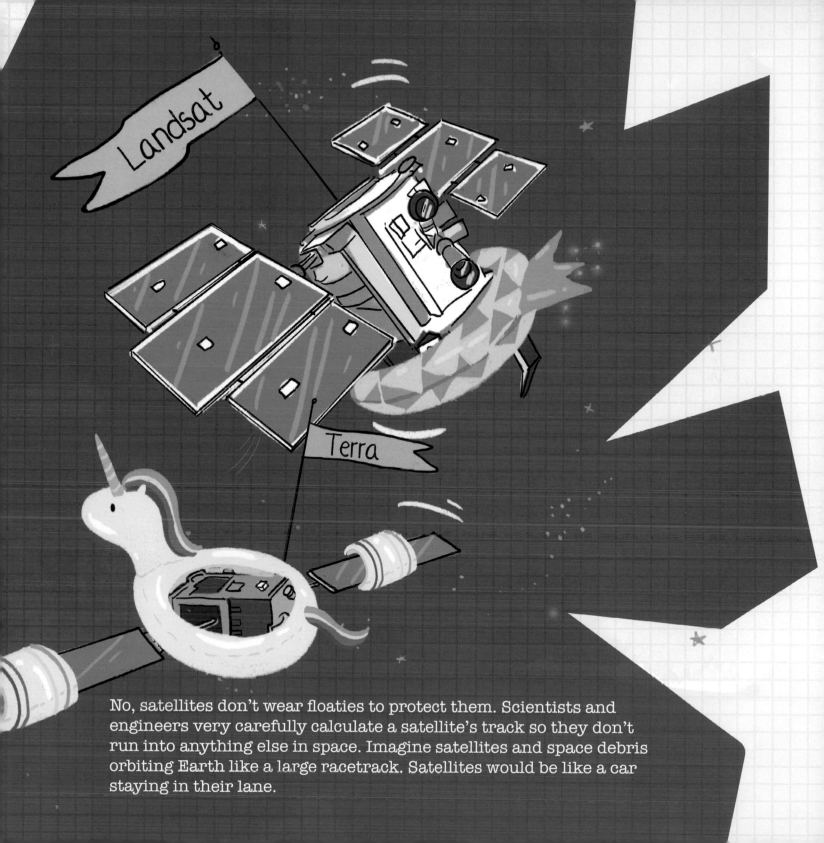

No, satellites don't wear floaties to protect them. Scientists and engineers very carefully calculate a satellite's track so they don't run into anything else in space. Imagine satellites and space debris orbiting Earth like a large racetrack. Satellites would be like a car staying in their lane.

There are thousands of satellites orbiting Earth, so it's a pretty busy racetrack. There is also lots and lots of space junk out there. Space junk refers to debris or broken-down satellites in space. This debris no longer serves any function, but with so much space junk, it's becoming more of a challenge to avoid collisions. Most space junk is small—really small. Some researchers estimate there are about 20,000 pieces that are the size of a softball or larger, about 500,000 pieces that are the size of a marble, and millions of pieces that are even smaller than that.

Occasionally objects orbiting Earth do get out of their lane. If there is a chance a satellite would hit another satellite or space junk, scientists can send a signal to a satellite to do an avoidance maneuver. To do this, thrusters on the satellite move it to a slightly different lane which allows it to avoid the collision.

Space junk is typically not bigger than a softball or marble!

How do scientists fix satellites
once they are in space? Do they send
space handy workers?

No, they don't send handy workers into space,
though that would be a job with a great view! If there
is a problem with the software on a satellite, engineers can
send a patch of computer code to the satellite to hopefully fix
the problem. If there is a physical problem with a satellite, that's
another story. Satellites are too far away to fix when they are in
space. That's why scientists and engineers work together to do lots
of testing before launching new satellites into space.

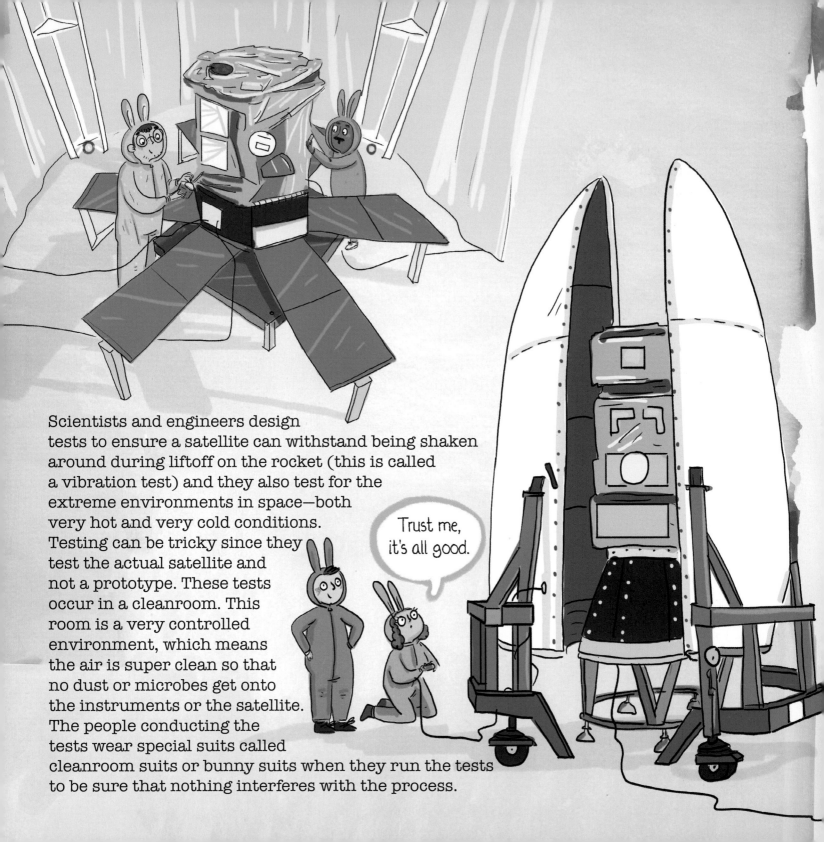

Scientists and engineers design tests to ensure a satellite can withstand being shaken around during liftoff on the rocket (this is called a vibration test) and they also test for the extreme environments in space—both very hot and very cold conditions. Testing can be tricky since they test the actual satellite and not a prototype. These tests occur in a cleanroom. This room is a very controlled environment, which means the air is super clean so that no dust or microbes get onto the instruments or the satellite. The people conducting the tests wear special suits called cleanroom suits or bunny suits when they run the tests to be sure that nothing interferes with the process.

Trust me, it's all good.

Scientists and engineers only get one shot at launching the satellite on a rocket, so they always triple check their tests and calculations.

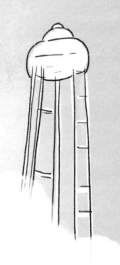

WHAT DO YOU WANT TO BE?

Satellites are an amazing example of how science, technology, engineering, and math come together. What part of the story of satellites excites you?

Do you want to be part of the research team, asking big scientific questions that set the focus for the mission? Maybe you want to know how sea levels are changing on Earth or maybe you want to research the landscape of other planets.

Research scientists identify what measurements or observations are needed to help answer their scientific questions.

RESEARCH SCIENTIST

Maybe you want to be part of the team that develops new technologies for instruments in space. Sometimes the observations or measurements needed to answer the science question require new technology. The instruments are going to be far away, and well, in space. Your everyday thermometer isn't going to cut it, so new instrument technologies are often developed.

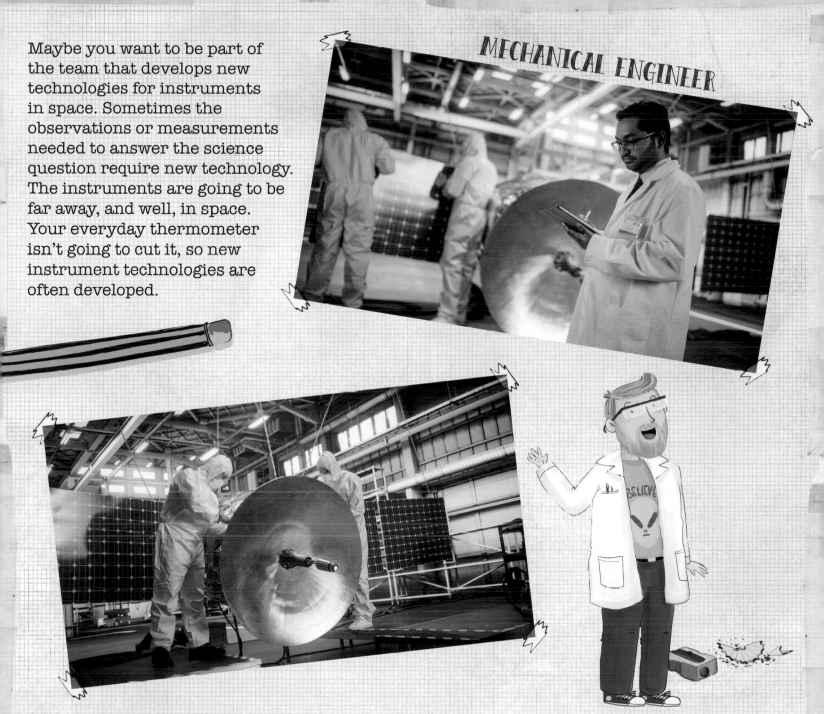

Mechanical engineers are responsible for developing the new technology, communication devices, powered devices, and all the tools satellites need when they are exploring space or collecting data.

AEROSPACE ENGINEER

Perhaps you are interested in building the satellite itself. The design of the satellite is also an exciting challenge since most satellites need to be compact inside the rocket then expand in space so that their solar arrays provide the satellite with power.

Aerospace engineers work to carefully design, build, and test each component of the satellite and make sure the whole thing can handle the rocket trip.

You know what they say, it is rocket science!

Maybe you want to be the one to process and analyze the data that comes back from satellites. Learning everything we can from the data instruments on satellites collect is important to improving our way of life on Earth and furthering exploration of space.

Remote sensing scientists take the data received from satellites and catalog it, analyze it, and use it to solve problems on Earth, learn more about space, and create new technology to get even more data!

REMOTE SENSING SCIENTIST

These are just some examples of what work can be done on a satellite. What interests you most?

It takes a lot of different people to get from the initial concept for the satellite to ultimately receiving data back from an operating satellite in space so that the data can be used to analyze the original research questions.

GLOSSARY

Antenna – an object that communicates with satellites in order to transmit information back to Earth

Astronaut – a person who travels into space in a spacecraft

Avoidance maneuver – an action a satellite takes to get out of the way of an object by changing course

Cargo – goods, merchandise, or anything else being transported

Cleanroom suits – outfits worn by scientists outside of their normal clothing to discourage contamination

Data – pieces of information or facts

Galaxy – a group of stars and other matter in outer space that is held together by gravity; Earth is located in a galaxy called the Milky Way

Gravity – the force that pulls objects together

Inertia – the tendency of objects to resist change to their current state of motion

Instrument – a tool or utensil, often used to aid in scientific endeavors

International Space Station – a spacecraft orbiting the Earth; provides astronauts with a place to live and work while researching outer space

Lidar – Light Detection and Ranging; similar to radar, uses a laser to measure speed, distance, direction, and other measurements of an object

Microbe – a very small organism

Momentum – the energy accumulated by a moving object

Moon – a natural, spherical object in outer space that orbits a planet

NASA – an acronym for National Aeronautics and Space Administration

Orbit – the path that an object follows while revolving around another object

Patch – code that is transmitted to a program to update its system or fix a mistake

Payload – satellites, people, and equipment transported by a rocket

Pollution – the release of substances (such as trash and chemicals) that harm the Earth

Propellant – a type of fuel used by spaceships to move forward by releasing mass backwards

Prototype – an early version of an object or machine; often used as a model to base future versions on

Radar – Radio Detection and Ranging; a tool used to measure various readings of an object, including speed, distance, and direction

Radio signal – a radio wave that is sent or received

Remote sensor – an instrument that detects energy or gathers other information about an object without physically interacting with the object

Rocket – an object used to launch spacecraft into outer space

Satellite – a type of machine that orbits Earth, taking pictures and collecting information

Solar array – a collection of solar panels that absorb sunlight to produce solar power

Solar power – a form of renewable energy produced by absorbing sunlight

Space junk – debris that exists in space that is made up of various human-made objects

Topography – a landscape's physical features

Universe – the entirety of outer space

Vibration test – a trial performed to approximate how much rapid movement an object can endure without being damaged

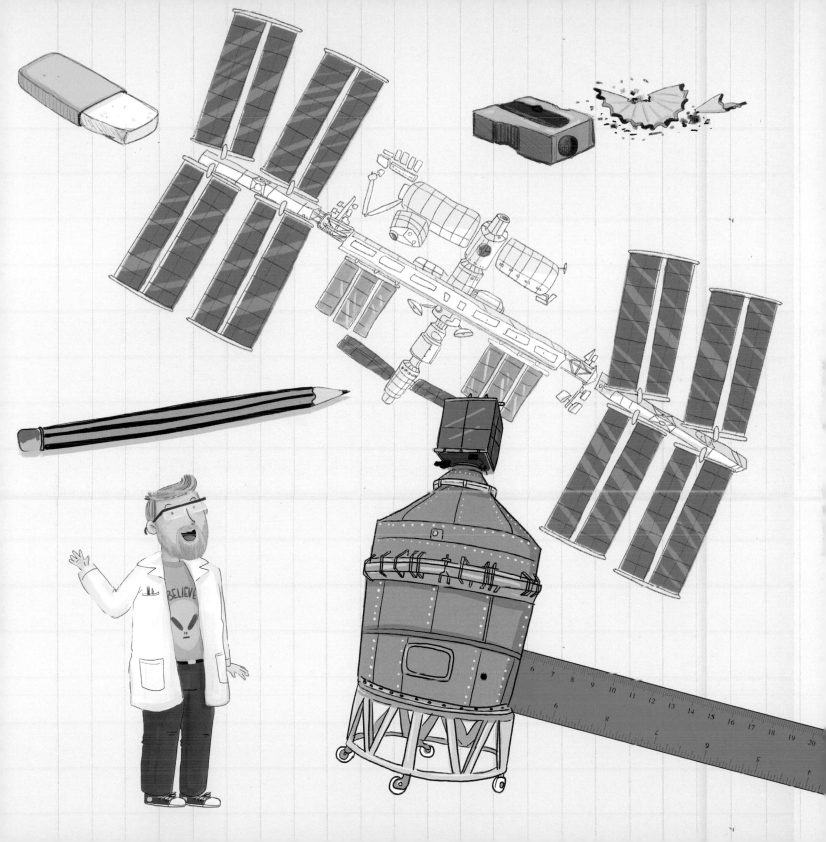